Light Through the Leaves:
Reflections on the Everyday Sacred

Gene Serianni

DEDICATION

To mom: who was the first to read most of these poems
Alyssa: who told me I should put them in a book
Christina: who started me writing again after so many years.

CONTENTS

1.

WHISPERS OF THE FALLS

Have you ever gone out on a hike
Come across a waterfall you did not know was there
Taken a few moments to sit down
And enjoyed what it had to share?

How the colors of the sun and foliage change
In the reflection of the falling water
And change again in the pool at the bottom
And transfer yet again as the water passes out of range,

Listen to the water rumble and trickle
As it dances about the stones
Sort of like the water is playing
Laughing and giggling as it roams,

Have you let the falls overtake your thoughts
For just a few moments, it has encompassed your mind
Taken away your worries and cares
So, stop and enjoy what a waterfall has to share.

2.

THE STORM NATURE SHARED

Have you ever sat on an open porch
During a heavy thunderstorm
Let the thunder chase out
The nagging thoughts that never go away?

Throw any angers
Put them in the streaming water
Watch them flow away
Throw your worries into the big raindrops,

They will flow along with your anger
Let your mind start to relax
Till the water finally stops.

The lightning flashes, leaving a bit of awe
Thunder comes crashing, making many bawl
But if we accept it as a friend
It can make all our problems small.

If you do, you may find, as the storm travels on
Sun following in its wake,
You may find yourself relaxed
And thank Mother Nature that day.

3.

A FATHER'S QUIET PRIDE

I remember when we brought you home
Soft and warm and wiggly
I watched as you started to grow
Smiling, giggling, and bubbly,

You went to school and learned so much
Reading and writing so ably
You made friends and grew so fast
No longer my little baby,

My pretty little girl grew up quickly
Through anguish and illness
We were able to make each other laugh
Helping each other through so much
Sometimes just vaguely,

You kept on working through school
Earning honors and my admiration
Completing so many things while growing inside
Becoming a wonderful young lady.

Most fathers will tell you how proud
They are of the grown-up babies
But I have always wanted to tell you
What an honor it is
To have you as my loving baby girl!

4.

THE MAKING OF US

How did we become who we are?
As you read these words
You are who you are now
Do not worry
If you want, you can still change.

Do you try to pet every dog you see
Or would you feel better away in a tree
Do you hide when you see a mouse
Or just live and let it be?

What words did you hear
That shaped your thoughts
What actions did you witness
That taught you the way to react?

The way you see the world
The way you treat others
The way you treat yourself
The way you see your future.

Have no worries or frets about it
If you like you, there is no need to change
If you are bothered by who you are, there is time to change
If you want to be more, a higher ceiling you can still attain.

5.

REFLECTIONS WITHIN

How many times have we asked ourselves
Am I doing the right thing
Did I do what I should have
Should I be doing this another way?

Have you ever said to yourself
This is not going well
Could this have come out better
Or the other way would have been better?

There is a time in our lives
When we use the knowledge we have accrued
Make decisions from what we know and have learned
And accept the results of things we do.

For better or worse
If those things were started with good intentions
Hoping to reach a higher finish
Though we might regret the ending
It all started with good wishes
To end with a positive view.

6.

FRAMED BY THE WINDOW

Look outside of the window
Let your mind take a picture
Is it interesting enough to store it
Or should your mind delete it and save the space?

Did you see a field of grass with multiple colors
Or maybe some trees sway in a breeze
Did you look out that window before
But things not seem the same things you see?

Have you looked out and seen a building
What color were the windows and walls
What color were the sidewalks and trees
Or maybe you can see a cityscape
Was it neat?

Did you see clouds about
With different colors and shapes
Or maybe you saw the dark of night
With spots of glowing light scattered about its scape.

Maybe you saw the midst of clouds
While traveling in a plane
The tops rolling up and down
Surrounded by the sky in different shades
All around.

Was it the window on a train
Going across the countryside
With fields, and crops, and animals about
Can you remember – has your mind tried?

Light Through the Leaves:

Or on a mountain road with sights
Like rocks, trees, and streams
Plants, animals, or even roadside rails
The sun poking between trees, making spotty gleams.

If you do not think looking out a window important,
Try being in a room or transportation without one
No way to see the passing of time, or distance
It also keeps people reminded of their own existence.

7.

THE WANDERING VESSEL

Have you ever felt yourself
Like a ship wandering at sea
The crew, the people who surround your life
Some good, some okay, some you wish you could flee?

Searching for a port to spend most of your days
Things going on about you that can put you at ease
More celebration moments than those full of strife
And other happenings that help you be at peace,

It may be impossible to find such a place
Like a utopia which will never be
Does that mean you will search all your days
I believe we are all destined to find the special place.

8.

Echoes of the Mind

I do not know the first time we met
But I do remember early memories
Visiting your home, meeting my cousins
Learning about my family tree,

You shared stories of great uncles and aunts
Some of whom I would never get to meet
Stories about my father growing up
Things he would never tell to me

I cannot tell when the stories became the same
Not remembering what you had told me
I do not know, you could not tell
Which nephew I was, and my daughter, your great niece.

It seemed all of a sudden at times
You did not know where in time and place you were
And snap, you know it instantly
"When," "where," and "how" were back
But now, infrequently,

In my heart and mind
Your care and kindness are always there
But no longer in my presence can you be.

9.

BECOMING LOVE

When did I know I loved you
It is probably not the right thing to ask
Having known you for such a long time
As children, we played like siblings
Not seeming to grow too fast,

Then the world seemed to change
Our lives seemed to get much larger
Our paths forward widened our lives
With our thoughts reaching farther ranges.

Thoughts of you were still there
Only seeing you every now and again
When I got to be in your presence
The moments seemed more special
Making me sure there was love for you,

Yet our paths traveled farther apart
As we found our ways through life
They crossed every now and again
Sometimes in laughter, sometimes in strife,

As moments of loneliness arrived
Our lives began to touch again
As I learned your struggles and *changes*
The torn pieces of love began to mend
And "love" became "in love"
Not just a friend.

10.

LESSONS WE MISSED

When did we learn we are different
When did we learn we are not like others
When did we learn we have different colors
From our eyes, to our hair, to our skin?

When did we learn we are pretty or plain
When did we learn we are handsome or homely
When did we learn we are short or tall
When did we learn we are thick or thin
How we look to others around us

When did we learn we are good or bad
When did we learn we are rich or poor
When did we learn we are nice or mean
When did we learn we are excitable or serene
How we look at ourselves?

When did we learn we are loving or indifferent
When did we learn we are giving or greedy
When did we learn we are peaceful or troublesome
When did we learn we are better or worse
In the way we treat others?

So, when will we learn to
Treat, see, and be to others
The way we wish to be?

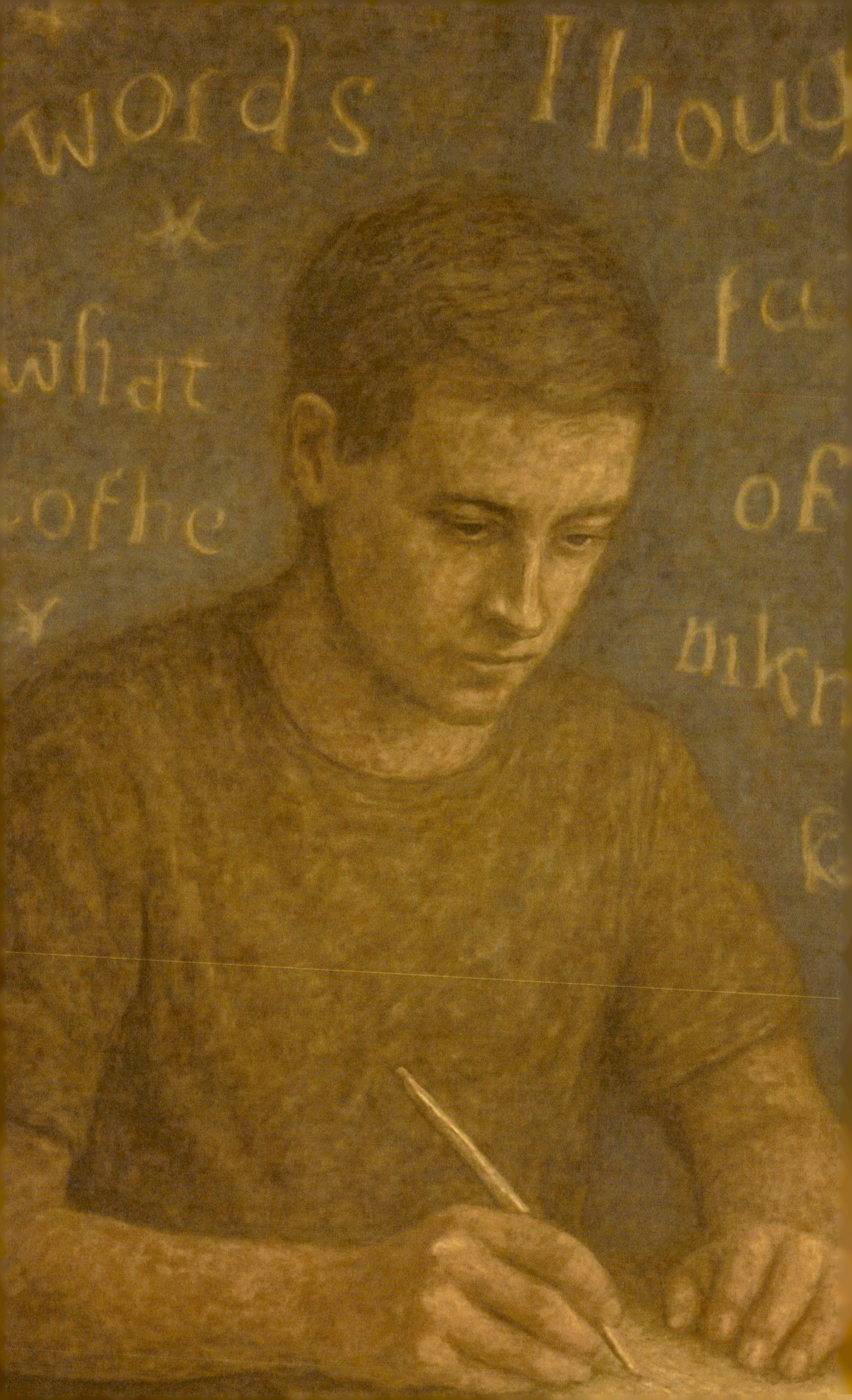
words
what
of

11.

FROM THOUGHT TO MEANING

Do you even wonder if the words you wrote
Mean the same to those that read them
Written words do not contain the inflections
That your mind assigned them as you write.

Will their reading change the context
Or the sentence's meaning?
Will they read that phrase
With a completely different leaning?

To you, your thoughts are clear
Even poignant in their meaning
That the reader may take it in a different direction
It is impossible, *you think*,
Because the words in your mind are so near?

Yet, write, you must in the way you feel
That it will be understood
In the meaning and manner you wrote it
And hope the reader can find how it came from your mind.

12.

LEANING INTO SUMMER

Have you ever sat on a roof or balcony
In the early summer
Feel the warmth of the sun
Toasting you just right to relax?

Birds go from chirping to singing
Smells turn to fragrances
Street snarls become gentle sounds.

You start to wonder how long you can hide here
Eventually, knowing you will be discovered
Maybe you can take a bit of what you found
Save it for the right moment
When you feel surrounded by the world
And use it to find a bit of serenity,

Not to hide forever, just every now and then
To ease life's intensity.

13.

NOURISH THE SPIRIT

Have you ever walked through the woods
Come across an open field
With tall grass catching bits of sun
Wild flowers of many colors
Emanating their fragrant scents?

Catch a glimpse of an animal's tail
Maybe a deer scampering off
A squirrel climbing through the trees
As birds winging from limb to limb,

The tall grass sways a little bit
Maybe because of a gentle wind
Or as it moves about
From small, unseen critters
Scurrying about near its roots,

So, if you walk through the woods
Take your ears and eyes.
Capture all around you
And take your soul to feed on nature's bounties.

14.

REMEMBERED MUSE

I never really thought about writing again
Seems I had lost my muse
Not really knowing where or when
Nor realizing I store away all these views,

Bottled up the connections between places
Objects and feelings
Blocking emotions linked to what is seen
Harkening back to who knows when.

Was it to avoid painful memories
Yet, none come to mind
Maybe it was to escape emotions
Though no uncomfortable feelings of any kind.

Maybe it is just the positive thoughts
That I have found all around me
Or an inner peace that came upon me
How it has come to me, I know naught.

But accept it with happy terms
I have come to do
And hope I have found a relaxed reader
To share my thoughts and views.

15.

ALTITUDE OF THOUGHT

Have you ever camped high in the mountains
Just below the tree line?
Drank from a run-off stream, clear and fine
Snow melted from the hill's cap of snow and ice.

The air is clean and unmuddied
No smug, exhaust, or mugginess
Rains come sometimes, not even reaching the ground
Even when it does, it can dry without the sun.

But do beware, the air is thin
No heavy lifting or running around
It gets very cold at night
Less animals and insects to make sounds.

The star so close you can almost pull one down
The skies so clear with nary a person near
Long views of white, green, and brown
Barely more than an empty mind's playground.

It seems wrong to speak out loud
Or leave something that wasn't here
Just accept the solitude you found
And the memories are forever dear.

16.

NATURE'S DESIGN

How does Mother Nature decide
What it will share with us and when
What flower will bloom, which petals it spreads
Or which colors it will blend?

Which birds will be around
Which animals will appear from underground
Where the reptiles will live *where*
What creature will forage here or there?

What all these creatures will eat
How each reacts when they meet
Which will live in fresh water
And which will live in the salty sea?

It tells some to live by the shores
Near oceans, lakes, or streams
Others near mounts or deserts
So, they have the cold or heat it needs.

People have tried to change these things
But will hardly ever succeed
Maybe we just have to learn
To leave Mother Nature be.

17.

THE LIGHTHOUSE ALONE

Alone on your pedestal of rock
Protected so many at night
And even through wicked storms
Awed and intrigued more in the light,

Each painted with its own color lines
Yet, only using a few different colors
Letting sailors know where they are sailing
So, no matter how rough the seas giving calmer minds,

You survive ocean storms
Life dedicated to the seas
Led many to romanticism
Even in the strong breezes,

Shown so many a beacon through the dark
Survived nature's many seasons
Yet no longer needed with today's navigation aids
You will have no mention except on historical pages,

Though your purpose is not needed to save
You will remain in our romantic thoughts
Have a new need by us to help guide us
Through dreams of ages long forgotten.

18.

LAYERS OF BECOMING

How did I become me
The days of my parents shaping my thoughts
The adults around me taking me this way and that
The teachers reading and teachings
The books read through the years
The movies absorbed by my mind
The songs heard affecting in kind,

Years of watching things around me
The giving by some, the taking by others
The hate, disdain, and angers of others
The hope, the caring, and the kindness around,

I have worked my way through it all
Tried to find the outlook that fits me best
The lack of need to judge others
The desire to help without stutter
And the self-acceptance to be myself.

19.

VOICES LEFT UNHEARD

I so wonder what you see
And how you see it
What you smell
And how do you categorize it?

I have seen the frustration in your eyes
And on your face
The confusion there as well
When others cannot understand what thoughts
You try to convey to us.

Your mind seems to have absorbed
So many things
And filed it away as only you can
I feel it our weakness not to understand.

Maybe we need a translator
To explain your actions and thoughts
To help you find the words you have naught.

I pray you find the way
To express to us who you are
And then to be accepted as such
So beyond what we had thought.

20.

THE SHAPE OF LOVE

For many of us, our first definition of love
Came from the people who raised us
They seemed to reach our emotions
To shape our words and thoughts,

To some, it is the companionship
Of our friends as we grow up
The shared thoughts and actions
That glued us together, whether rain or shine,

Some, it was the first time
We found that special one
The person in the first thought of a day
And often also the final one,

Or maybe the person whose image
Appears to us throughout the day
Their words and actions on our minds
The person who comes to mind during the quiet times,

Searching inside ourselves to find
What makes us happy
And fills us with calm and joy
No wonder it is hard to define
Or ever so hard for us to find.

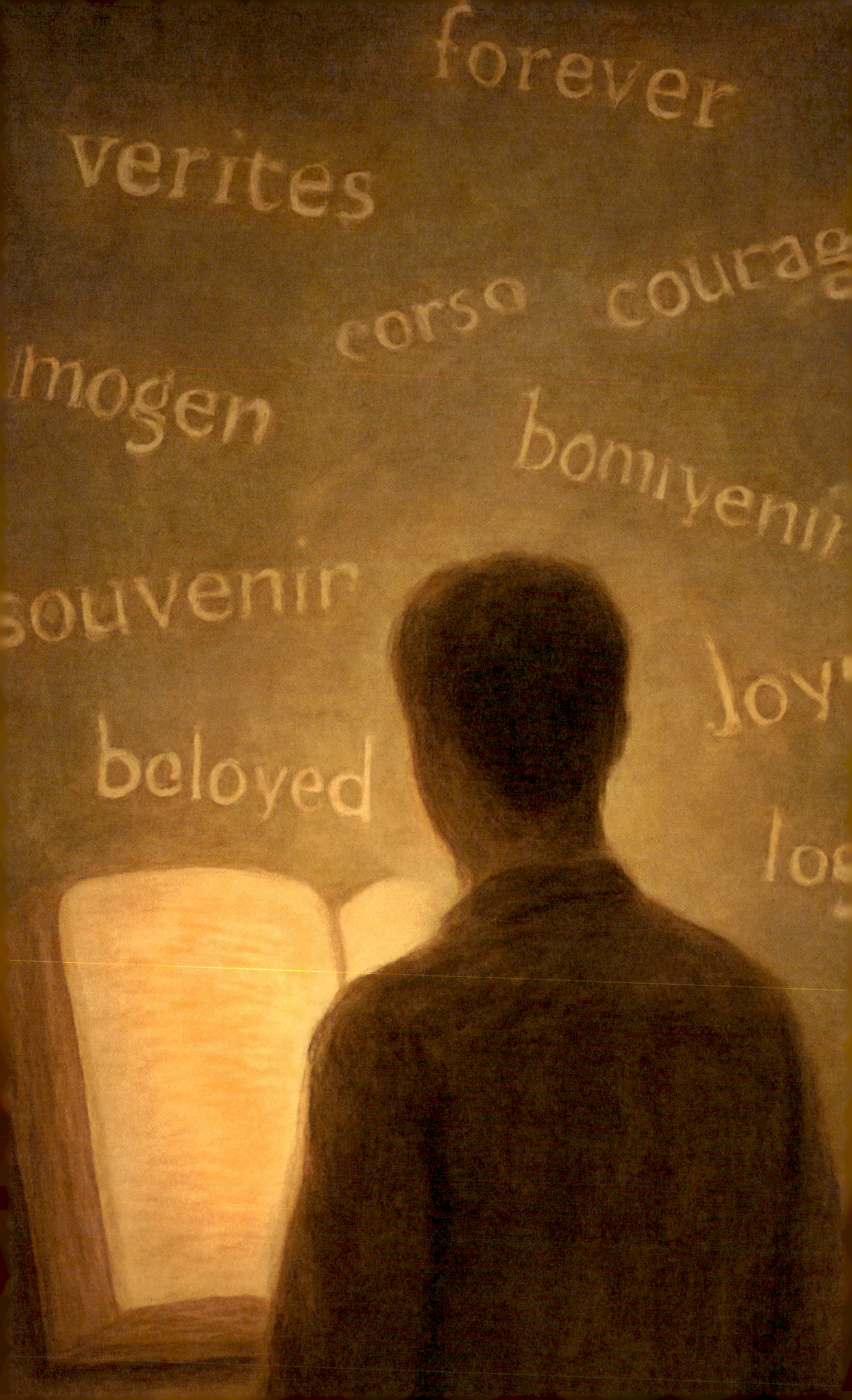
forever
verites
corso
souvenir
beloved

21.

WORDS THAT STAY

Some people have no idea how far
What they do can reach
While sometimes people try on purpose
To cause the behavior of the past be breached,

Say some words in front of a small group
Speaking words to be understood
Give a speech in front of a large group
Hoping what is said is believed,

Proclaim loudly, how many will listen
To all the words that are said
Talk softly, how many will seem to care
Would the words be better absorbed instead?

Reactions can go on for years
Phrases quoted for many generations
Behaviors changing after what was said
And perhaps even tears will be shed.

So, speak your thoughts and feelings
Who knows how it would be heard or received
But rest assured, after you are done
Your mind and soul will be relieved.

22.

MEASURING TIME

Have you stolen any of it yet
Has it gotten away from you
Have you finished it
Or have you run out of it?

Is it yours yet
Or is it someone else's
Are you waiting for some extra
Or have you decided to give up on it?

It tells us how long to play
And tells us how long to rest
Let us know when to wake up
And when to go to sleep.

We ask it to go faster
Sometimes to slow down
No matter what we want of it
It travels as it always has.

We will never learn to
Live without it
We have to learn to
Resign ourselves,

Because time is always itself.

23.

SAILING LIGHTHEARTED

Have you ever sat astride the bow of a boat
Your hair, being blown about
Hearing nothing but lapping waves
And flapping of any loose cloth that is about?

The sight of the sail pushed tight
The sail stretched from boom to mast
Straining out the starboard side
The boat, being hurried on its run,

Center board is up
Nothing lowered to slow it down
Anything dragging is pulled up inside
Those inside the boat thrilled by the ride,

Have you sat at the stern
Watch as *someone strains against the tiller*
To keep it in the sweet spot
On the invisible line the wind has made?

All too soon, the time will come
Some ducking the boom as the boat comes about
Down comes the center board
Someone pushing hard against the tiller,

A fulfilling ride, so silent
And much too short
Lining up to do it again
What a funny sport!

24.

THROUGH YOUR EYES

Looking through those windows of blue
Knowing the years that sit behind
Hoping the mind that is with it
Still thinks of me in kindness or is fond.

I think of the moments I get to see
Those eyes and that face, other than in my mind
They are too short and far in between
To bring ease to my lonely mind,

I hope the days ahead will bring
These things closer to my being
Because they are already
Held tightly in my heart and mind.

25.

IN THE WILDERNESS OF SELF

Have you ever gone hiking
Up a mountainside
Looked down from the edge of a cliff
Or looked beyond from the mountain top?

Hiked through a wooded area
Going along an animal trail
Looking for birds and squirrels in the trees
And hearing the whisper of the wind rustling leaves,

Have you hiked around a lake
Seen different plants and flowers at its side
Found its feeder creek, mud on either side
And found the right rocks to help, cross it dry?

Hiked through a city
Crossed sidewalks and streets
Hear people talk and play
Spreading the news of the day,

Let's go hiking and see
How our world gets bigger today.

26.

TO CAMP, TO BREATHE

Have you ever camped in the woods near a lake
Felt the breeze over the water across your skin
Watched the reflection of a sunrise upon its surface
Or the reflection of the sunset - *such alike effect?*

Watched water birds land and alight
Or watched people frolicking in the sunlight?

Have you ever camped along a beaten wooded trail
Listen to the wildlife trapsing in the woods
Or a woodpecker tapping out its song
Heard the trees groan as they rub in the wind
Or smelt the seasons' foliage, the breeze stirring about?

Have you camped near an ocean
Breathing in the sea's fragrance
Heard the waves lapping at sand and stone alike
Or heard the seabirds cry, inviting their friends
Or felt the sea's breeze changing the air's dampness?

Have you camped near a mountain top
Felt the warmth leave with the sun
Had the weather change by the moment
Watched how fast the world lightens up with the rising sun
Or how quickly it darkens as it drops behind the edge of the next ridge?

Try some camping if you desire
To learn nature's many faces
It can help lead your heart and soul
To so many different places.

27.

FIRELIT REMEMBRANCE

Sitting around a campfire
Watching its flames dance about
Close enough to feel its warmth
Yet far enough away not to melt,

Roasting marshmallows above the flames
Trying to keep it high enough
To not catch fire again.

Cooking hot dogs skewered on a stick
Getting it close enough to a cook
But far enough so it doesn't taste torched

Watching its glow so calming and near
The crackling and hissing and playing
Like a lullaby melody,

Sliding into sullenness
Just about ready to sleep
Taken over by slumber deep.

28.

MIND BEYOND JUDGMENT

Have you ever wished
That others were more like you
Liked the foods you did
Watched the movies you enjoyed
So their thoughts you could understand.

Or maybe you want to be like them
Always find clothes you like
And get to play games to enjoy
Avoid any arguments because they think the same,

Maybe it would be best
If you learned to understand yourself -
Enjoyed your similarities and differences
And add your uniqueness to life
In turn, it makes you part of many.

29.

SOUNDTRACK OF THE CITY

City sounds can vary from street to street
And from neighborhood to neighborhood
Some familiar and some unique,

The sound of cars and trucks
Shared throughout the town
Yet the sound of children
Laughing and playing, much more rare.

The sound of music is found
Almost everywhere
But the type and volume
Many not be a familiar fare,

Some areas have creeks and woods
With the sounds of birds and animals around
Some have trees and leaves
Rustling and swaying
Some are stone and brick work
Making the sounds echo from between.

Some even have fountains
Sounds of bubbling and splattering arise
The sound of a city can be such a surprise.

30.

THE LOYAL COMPANION

Have you ever had that pet
That seemed to read your mind
Seemed to snuggle when you are sad
Or in a melancholy mood?

Or knew when you felt happy
When to be playful and cheery
Being quiet by your side when your mind is working
And sharing a few bites of food when you are snacking.

Pets come in so many shapes and sizes
Lizards, snakes, and dogs
Cats, birds, and horses
Just the animal that has earned your trust and love
Whose presence can make almost anywhere
One of your favorite spaces.

31.

SEA OF MEMORY

Looking out upon the ocean
To where the sea and sky meet
Standing barefoot at the edge of the beach
Feeling the waves turn to ripples on my feet,

I cannot tell if it is cold or warm
I would need to wander further into the sea
At least as far as to let the water
Reach both the front and back of my knees.

Watching the surf roll into a bubbly froth
Seeing waves break out further
See white caps at the apex of the wave
Then, under the wave, the foaming will roll,

Under which life unseen
Like fish and crab, seaweed and shark
Maybe a few mammals like dolphins or whales around
Very few of them ever make a sound.

No matter near or far
The ocean keeps life around us
And so few of us stop to see
My memories would be so different
Without the bounding sea.

32.

MEASURED BY THE WORLD

How does society come to decide
What each person is worth?

A news reporter who read what is written
An investigator that collects information
An editor who decides how best to distribute it?

Or an athlete who excites the fans
A manager who picks which athlete is best for his team
A coach who teaches and directs the athlete to their best effect
Or the owner who pays them and keeps them together
And the fans who cheer and pay to keep them around?

Or teachers who teach knowledge
And try to shape students' behaviors
The secretaries that collect information
And try to find the best way to share in each situation
The principles that try to bring guidance
And order to it all?

What of builders, repair people
And all the trades that make living in the modern world possible
Scientists, academics, artists, writers
Technicians, programmers, inventors
The list goes on and on
Many complete a job even at times while others scorn.

So how do we decide the worth?
No fans, no jobs, no athletes
No sick people, no work for doctors
No cashiers, no way to buy the things we need
To make life a bit more livable.

Light Through the Leaves:

Farmers for food, so much unspoken
The world needs all to keep going
But who is worth the most?

Maybe the true measure of worth
Is set by each of us, for better or worse
There is no one encompassing formula
No one answer.

Everyone plays a part
The best way they know how to
Let the world measure, but be sure you know
Everyone has an importance to someone
Even to people unknown.

33.

VOICE ON THE PAGE

To write a few words
Or to share a new thought
To convey some emotion
Or explain a dream beyond what is taught.

Have you written a poem
Or a story or two
Read a book in silence
Or watched a movie with a crew?

Tell how you felt
The fears and angers
Draw a picture with your words
Whether in happiness or anguish?

You can write your thoughts
With pictures or with words
Show your thoughts and feelings
They are important even in such a large world.

So, draw your picture
Or write down your words
You can share them with others
Or keep them for yourself
Just remember…they are important
Because there is no one like yourself.

34.

SUNLIT GRATITUDE

Thank you, Mr. Sun
As you climb out of your blanket of night
And show us the beginning of the day's light
I wait in wonder for the first sign of today,

Watching how you change the sky
How you will paint the clouds of charcoal, white, and gray
The subtle but brilliant hues of orange, purples, and beige?

And yet I can never be sure
If you do it on purpose or tease
Or what might come for us this day.

You can fill the sky with colors
Sometimes sharply, others a haze
It could be just in a corner
Yet, others filling every space.

For a moment, you change the colors
Of things here and in space
Holding me for a moment in one place
Never really knowing how long you arrested my gaze,

I can then thank you, Mr. Sun
For such a warm start to my day.

35.

HER RISE AGAIN

I do not remember the moment you changed
From a giddy, smiling, and playful girl
To a wide-eyed, still smiling young lady,

Nor the moment you became to me
An intelligent, soulful young woman
Still having that wonderful smile,

I can remember when I saw you
A beautiful, warm-hearted, and graceful young lady
Still with that wonderful smile.

Yet, the next time we met, you were just a shell
Eyes showing frustration, loneliness, and fear of the unknown
Worse yet, missing that wonderful smile,

Then, I saw it start to arrive in you
With determination, motivation and confidence
But mostly, I noticed the return of that wonderful smile.

You are now a lady not afraid
With charm, caring, and quiet elegance, continuing to thrive
And it seems here to stay again
That WONDERFUL SMILE.

36.

MEMORIES, DISTILLED

Why can memories be so strange
They are the mind's recordings of yesterdays
We remember the hard parts fairly well
We remember the good parts fondly,

Yet, the spaces of time between such events
It seems hard to recollect them all
Do we remember them in chronological order
No matter, they occurred in spring, winter, or fall.

I often wonder if that is how it happened
Or does my mind dress them up a bit
Did it occur as they are remembered
Or just as we wanted them to be?

I guess it doesn't really matter
Once they are in my mind, they will not change
Some even seem no more than a dream
But who can change what the mind has arranged?

37.

SPRING'S AWAKENING

Went through the park today
Spring seemed to put on a show
Trees blooming with leaves
Of yellows and greens, from dark to light
Reds, pinks, browns, and white
Even a painter would have it rough today.

Bushes and plants are chiming in
Fuchsias, purples, reds, and greens
All seem more brilliant
Reflecting the glowing daylight,

The stream trickling softly
Could not even call it a babbling brook
Birds stooping to drink a bit thirstily
While squirrels play from rock to tree,

People walking quietly, enjoying all we see
It is amazing how such a day
Can adjust the things we will feel and say,

Do not worry if you missed it
There are sure to be many more
But I had to share today's
It is one of many things I adore.

38.

CURTAIN OF LIGHT

Come, sit with me and watch
As the warm summer day comes to a close
Watch the water lap at the shores
Or the sunlight crinkle on the wakes,

See the sea grass bend and stand
As the breeze rakes across the marshes
We are about to watch a show that changes
Almost every day, come what may.

The sun continues its journey through its day
Slide smoothly to the horizon across the bay
Finding cloud, both seen and not so obvious
Painting them multi-colors - almost none are gray.

Even the sky itself seems to lose its blue hues
Filling it with pinks, oranges, reds and maroons
Even the wind joins in with sounds
Playing tunes with the leaves and reeds,

Such a wonderful show
Nature puts on for us!

39.

MOUSE OF MIGHT

Hello, little fellow gray and white
So meek and shy
Quiet both day and night
Ye people fear you
As if you were full of might,

I know you are out and about
Seeking the substance of water and food
Scurrying from here to there
Barely the size of a thumb
You could just as well be a bear,

You can make people run
While you scurry about the place
Running from you as if you were
Made from poison or mace.

Inside or outside, you may roam
Looking for nothing more than
Food or a home
Seeking only freedom and nothing more.

Just a word of advice
To you, Mister Mouse:
People will always chase you
When you visit their home or house.

40.

Gray Morning Hope

No sunrise to be seen this day
But still up and moving about
The sky filled with dark and light gray
Daytime duties still happen anyway,

Maybe a bit less cheerful
The tone not as carefree and gay
Yet happy to be up and moving
Better than lazing around all day,

Maybe a little rain may fall
Or a wind to chase clouds away
Moving about will change none of this
Or being over-cheerful will change what we feel or say.

The chance to be moving is more than something
For there are some who do not have this choice
Whether due to illness or disability
Some without a voice or say.

I am glad for each moment I have
Though I may not think of it every day
I am willing to deal with life
No matter what it brings each day.

41.

A Mindful Day

Have you ever noticed
How a day starts, so it seems to go
A pleasant sight and a pleasant thought
Then the day seems to go pleasantly from dawn to dusk,

Yet a day that starts gray
With maybe fog, snow, or rain
Can feel heavy with problems
And by the day's end, we feel drained,

Yet, there have been days starting with rain
But a pleasant thought filling my brain
These days seem to pass okay
But do not reach the level of a pleasant day.

But what of days that start blandly
From the beginning, heat and haze
I think it is up to us and our thoughts
To bring about a more pleasant day.

Maybe I have allowed myself
To be guided to the types of days
Maybe I should find a way
To see them as pleasant days.

Find a way to absorb good and bad
Soften them to gentle moments
Think kind and gentle thoughts
And believe evil is never meant.

42.

SNOW'S QUIET MOMENT

I was just sitting calmly
Absorbing a late spring heat
My mind deciding to take me away
To a winter's day not long ago
That was very unique,

If each thing had happened alone
Or even coming in pairs
I would have barely noticed
But all together it was rare.

As I walked out of the cabin
Sitting next to a high mountain lake
I noticed it was oddly warming up
The ice starting to melt without sunglare,.

The trees covered in frost
Evergreens covered in gray
Fogg surrounding the trees and lake
Sun barely peeking through reminding me it is day.

The only sight not gray
Was a black bear next to the lake
It was getting its first drink of the day
With me standing still till it meandered away.

Thank you, mind, for this little gift
Leaving me one other thing to say
I will enjoy this warmth
So long, I am off to play.

43.

NAMING THE COLORS

Who gave colors their names
Whether brilliant or dusky
Maybe bold or just tame
Who gave them their names?

Someone decided there were primary colors
Gave them each a simple name
Long before we were born
And people followed along like a rule to a game,

Then others started to mix them together
Changing the rules of the name game
Colors' names soon became complicated
Trying to create sights we cannot ignore.

Who decided blood was red
Or fields of grass are green
Roses can be red, pink, yellow, or white
Did you get what I've said so far
Do you understand what I mean?

Oceans are blue, so is the sky
Then people changed their portrayal of them
using paints and dyes
Started using colors to describe things
That have no such disguise.

Some things are red hot
Someone is feeling blue inside
I just want to meet these peoples
Just so I can ask them why.

44.

THROUGH THEIR EYES

How do we want others to see us
Just what do we want them to see
The clothes, the shape, the face, the eyes
Or the caring, sharing, and the love inside?

Maybe the combination of all this
What about us do we hope
They will concentrate their emphasis
Which aspect do we cherish most?

The heart and mind take longer to know
The clothes, hair, and shape are seen right away
But can also be paid for and bought
Yet heart and mind are not made that way.

Someone can arrange the outer shell
And hope it is all you will ever see
Not trusting their inner self is enough
To ensure these people can be seen.

I was lucky young in life
I started searching for what was within
No, there is nothing wrong with taking care
What is on the outside, it is neither a crime or sin.

But I chose to focus on the inside
Because that is where my happiness ends and begins.

45.

THE TURNING SEASONS

Life is always changing
Things evolve around us
Sometimes good, sometimes bad
There is nothing wrong with admitting
When they make us sad.

We often celebrate when
The changes make us happy
Get angry when they make us mad
It often garners emotions from thought we have.

People in our lives pass on
Others are newly born
Memories pass in thought
While the future grows on.

Just be accepting that things will change
That our challenges in life will continue on
It is how we react to the changes
That shape how we go on.

46.

REDIRECTED FEELING

Too often, I have met people
Who have told me I am under par
Whether it is my station in life
Or the way I look and dress
Or not behave the way they expect
When faced with moments of strife,

It took me time to realize
Their behaviors are often a sign
Of personal frustrations inside themselves
Or lack of self-confidence through life,

They find it safer
To strike out at others
Than to chance being discovered
For who they are inside.

Do not accept what they say as truths
For the only one that knows you
Your faults and your positives
Is the person who spends all their
Time with you.
 And that person is you.

47.

WIND AND MYSTERY

So, you are back again
No one can see you come
No one ever sees you go
No one knows if you are friend or foe.

Sometime you are kindly
Just kissing plants, flowers, and leaves
Other times a bit more forceful
Knocking things around and pushing things free.

You have assisted boats and ships that use canvas
And yet, you can hinder planes and jets
When you show the brutal you
You leave things everywhere, a frightful mess.

You are known by many names
Breeze, gust, wind, to name a few
You travel alone through the air
Other times, other times with rain, hail, sleet, and snow.

As much damage as you can cause
You are helpful and needed as well
So, thankyous and curses change as you do
But to live without you, I am sure we cannot.

48.

RIDE THROUGH ERAS

Have you ever ridden on a train
Not today's quiet, comfortable ride
With its clean, almost silent engine
Or cars that slide soft and smooth,

But ridin' in a Pullman car
Without the modern amenities
Where cooling comes from an open window
Heat from a potbellied wood or coal stove,

There were no high-backed plush seats
But bench seats whose back could flip to and fro
No quiet diesel electric engines
But a brutish steam engine - clunk, clank, and go.

To not get to see the stack billowing out
The trail of smoke drifting across the ground
The scenery goes by at a slow yet steady pace
The whistle blowing its throaty howl.

Watch animals startled but not scared
Like us watching a grumpy old man
Passing by them here and there
Having witnessed this time and again.

Take a ride if the chance comes around
The sights will differ from modern means
Feel how older generations may have crossed the ground
A way of life long passed its prime
But memories of things I have frozen in my mind.

49.

ANOTHER DAY OF EASE

Have you ever noticed
So a day starts, so it seems to go
A pleasant sight and pleasing start
The day then passes pleasantly from
Dawn to dark,

Yet, a day that starts gray
With maybe snow, fog, or rain
Can seem heavy with problems
And at the end of which we feel drained,

Yet, there have been mornings started with rain
But pleasant thoughts filled my brain
These types of days seem to pass okay
But not reach the level of pleasant days.

But what of the days that start blandly
Like fog or heat filled haze
I think it is then we should use our thoughts
To bring about more pleasant days.

Maybe I have allied myself
To be guided to types of days
So maybe I need to find a way
To see them all as pleasant days,

Find a way to absorb both good and bad
Soften them to gentle moments
Believe evil is never meant
And think kind and peaceful thoughts for days.

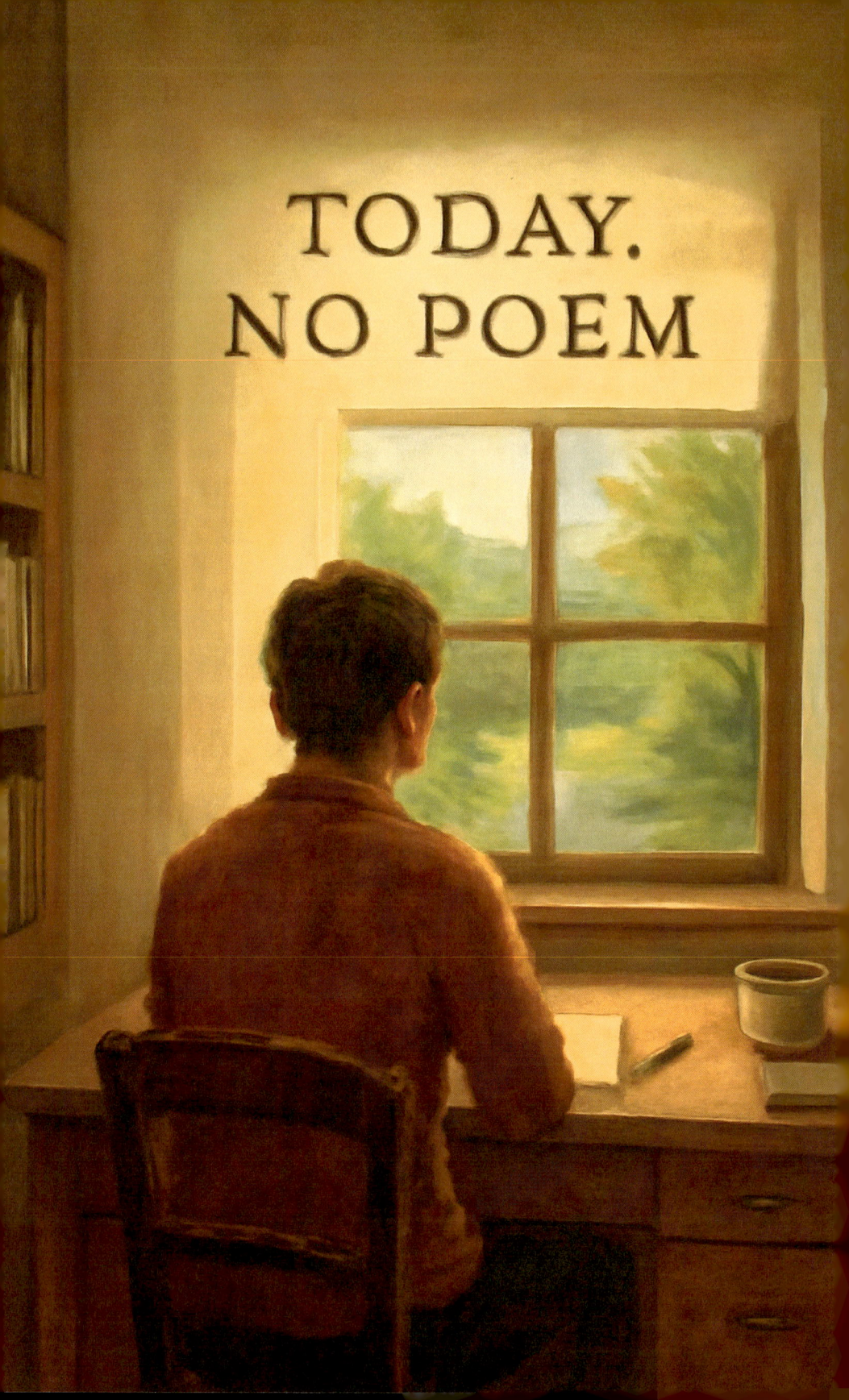

50.

TODAY, NO POEM

Someone just asked if I had a poem today
But my mind has no subject to explore
No true thoughts, nothing for it to say
No specific words to write, no subject to portray,

I had never known the muse will show
What subject or object will catch my fancy
Or where the pool or descriptions will grow
What next will make my mind and fingers dance?

There is so much in this world to share
Thoughts and feelings abound
But when have I matured enough
For my fingers to write them down,

I guess these words have earned a space
Found a need for me to expound
The words have gotten busy enough
To claim a section in my mind
And then, to paper to claim their place.

Strange, how the subject of no subject
Can cause a brain to stir
Mix together a recipe of words
Even though they never were.

51.

COMPANY IN SOLITUDE

Have you ever sat down alone
In a wooded area by yourself
Maybe on an old treestump or a large stone,
Taking time to think some thoughts?

How long did it take
Til you realized you were not alone
Memories of people who have passed on
Or thoughts of loved ones appear?

Maybe a beloved song visits your mind
Or a hated memory comes near
As long as you have thoughts and dreams
You can never be alone.

You can steer your thoughts
To happiness and cheer
But remember their nemesis
Are close by and near.

Absorb the moments that you have peace
Prepare yourself just in case
For not so fun thoughts that might appear
Be ready to send them to waste.

52.

LETTERS LEFT BEHIND

Have the days gone forever
When we would wait by the door
For the mail person to bring a letter
A correspondence from a friend or more?

Words written with care and elegance
Obviously, with thoughtful information
Giving us information we did not have before
Received in a mind provoking manner
Even thoughts we may abhor.

Writing with purpose and elegance
Sharing thoughts and dreams
With friends, loved ones, and relatives
With people we love and adore.

Now it is just texting
Quick thought that we often ignore
No more thoughtful sessions
Telling of love, heartache
 and moments we felt self-assured.

I miss the correspondences
Of stories and good intentions
It seems, in text, these things
Are hardly ever mentioned.

Bring back the art of letters
Full of information and love
Bring back the moments of anticipation
Of the times we waited for those to come.

53.

THE HEART'S DESIGN

If you thought this might help you understand
What love is or what it could be
I could not get there, but what I did
Was to learn to accept it, however it comes to me.

So many have been saying what it is like
Love can make you braver
Love can make you happy
Love can make you sad
Love can make you miss a person more.

There are many songs written about it
Love is a many splendored thing
Love is a drug I cannot live without
Love's light shines all around us
Even just a silly love song.

All these things make us think about love
But do not help us explain or describe it
Yet each of us believes we have an understanding
Of what they mean to teach us.

I have come to believe there are many levels of it
That there are many types of it
There are many chances to show it to others
Maybe even chances to share it as well.

I think there is love in us all
Just waiting to be shown and shared
And will come back to us in good measure
From others who can love and care.

54.

JOURNEY BEGINS HERE

Have you ever noticed
Getting to your vacation spot
Can be so stressful to start
Between the packing and the travel?

Loading the car and fighting the traffic
Usually, havoc and bedlam involved
Yet my memory recalls one trip
It sits in my mind as a singular occasion,

Long before GPS, we had maps
This trip, I looked them over seeking a quiet route
Finding a back highway to travel upon
Avoiding busy roads and towns to boot.

Even the weather seemed just right
Open windows with no A/C
I put in my homemade music CD
Starting cruising, refusing to get uptight.

Suddenly, I found myself singing along
Relaxed and moving at a decent clip
Mildly calm and more so with each song
It started to make me think:

Heck with the final destination
Wondering how far the fuel tank can take me
Maybe I can just keep cruising like this
And can I ensure a peaceful vacation trip?

SHARED HORIZON

55.

SHARED HORIZON

I am sitting here remembering
An early summer ride
Feeling the wind in my face
While I'm riding astride,

Hearing the engines' rhythmic rumble
Feeling the vibrations that coincide
The swaying that occurs on gentle curves
Calming the feelings I feel inside,

The sun's heat filtered by the trees
It's glare peeking through the leaves
Flickering off reflective surfaces
Leaving a warm, relaxing sight for me to see.

The flick of the wrist and squeeze of a hand
Sends the land by faster
Yet a tap of my foot and another squeeze
Will stop me from getting out of hand.

The persistent sounding rumble
Will put me in a relaxed state
Sometimes quickly sometimes slower
When the pilot inside determines the pace.

I miss the trips on my motor bike
Maybe get back to the riding
But will it measure up to the memories
Or show the unhappy parts they are hiding?

www.ingramcontent.com/pod-product-compliance
Lightning Source LLC
Chambersburg PA
CBRC090824120626
46547CB00007B/600